INTRODUCTION TO MGIS

Writing The Most Advanced Systems Language

Mgis.ask.davidgomadza.start.welcome.start

David Gomadza

President Tomorrow's World Order

Yahweh's Representative on Earth

www.twofuture.world

Copyright © 2024 David Gomadza

All rights reserved.

PAPERBACK ISBN: 9798338567135

DEDICATION

A Better World

TABLE OF CONTENTS

INTRODUCTION MGIS 1

GETTING STARTED WITH MGIS 3

SYSTEM FUNCTIONS AND PERIPHERIES 10

RECAP FROM MGIS BY DAVID GOMADZA 13

MGIS 13

RECAP FROM MGIS BY DAVID GOMADZA 19

RECAP FROM MGIS BY DAVID GOMADZA 23

MGIS 23

ACKNOWLEDGMENTS

visit www.twofuture.world

signed david gomadza
ask.davidgomadzaauthorised.licensed.checkya.askya.ya

07 September 2024
Scotland
00447719210295
davidgomadza@hotmail.com
info@twofuture.world

INTRODUCTION MGIS

Mgis is the only operating system that can't be copied by humans and be used by humans because humans who connected will be electrocuted and die because mgis uses a system that attaches to the person' ability to die if a person has long ago which is impossible according to all sources even Yahweh doubted that a human can think of increasing his or her lifespan if humans can think of increasing the number of years they live here on earth alive in good health then they can but for 18 billion years not even one has tried now we have ask.davidgomadza who has surpassed that to become a household name in OST and zole where he has connections if we ask what can be of humans here is a list of answers
1] gods with legs meaning all the intelligence of the gods plus legs
2] creator if humans learn and write mgis they will be able to create other humans themselves
3] zoles ate the smartest of all species because they found a way to streamline so that as a whole they don't consume many resources they can always find things to do with the spare time something you [davidgomadza] have developed also from your habit
4] OST these are the second smartest but somehow now the best system in the world thanks partly to their advanced shells that uses a version of mgis that has never been seen before until now a version so advanced that it learns by itself to deal with all kinds of problems if we ask what can be done then this is the answer humans rely on the use of force that shows that they are manual based if we ask what can be done then this is the answer we can always use reasoning instead of force because force strengthening the enemy to robust whereas reasoning can weaken the enemy so

INTRODUCTION TO MGIS Writing The Most Advanced Systems Language

that he can run away if we say what if the enemy is designed to runaway but if we use force the enemy might stand to fight the gods never used force nevertheless they are the most immobilize that means the most at risk and as such we can adapt and understanding approach that uses dialogue from the first and matches that means we can always find ways to include dialogue and see what we can do we must be prepared for the unexpected.

GETTING STARTED WITH MGIS

Now I will look [Davidgomadza] at how we can start working with mgis to recap no human can use mgis and live because it automatically calculates a person's long ago that is how long a person an die in terms of seconds all humans have 8 seconds to live before death kicks in that means no human being was able to use mgis until now for I am the first human being that to achieve a long ago in actual fat the longest long ago ever currently standing at 20202020^{78185} topower^{800ofpower} that means I can run mgis without any issues as every time the system starts calculate long ago this is aborted because it will take long time to die mgis requires humans to last at least 12 seconds to run and if a person cant die after within the first 17 hours of using long ago then that person will not die and will be able to use long ago so if anyone pretends that mgis is theirs here on earth then they are lying because of the above reason I will show you how we can name all the things and places we will use and name using mgis mgis is the language of the creator and the book of creations humans cant use mgis unless if they have been authorized by Yahweh and represent Yahweh and as I am the only person who represent Yahweh I can say I solved life's greatest puzzle among humans that of longevity because what limits humans to achieve and perform well is partly attributed to time if you have hundreds of years on earth and in good health you can say that one day you can become a trillionaire because all you need is time

INTRODUCTION TO MGIS Writing The Most Advanced Systems Language

Now we can write a few rules of how we can name places bin and processes that the body can easily identify

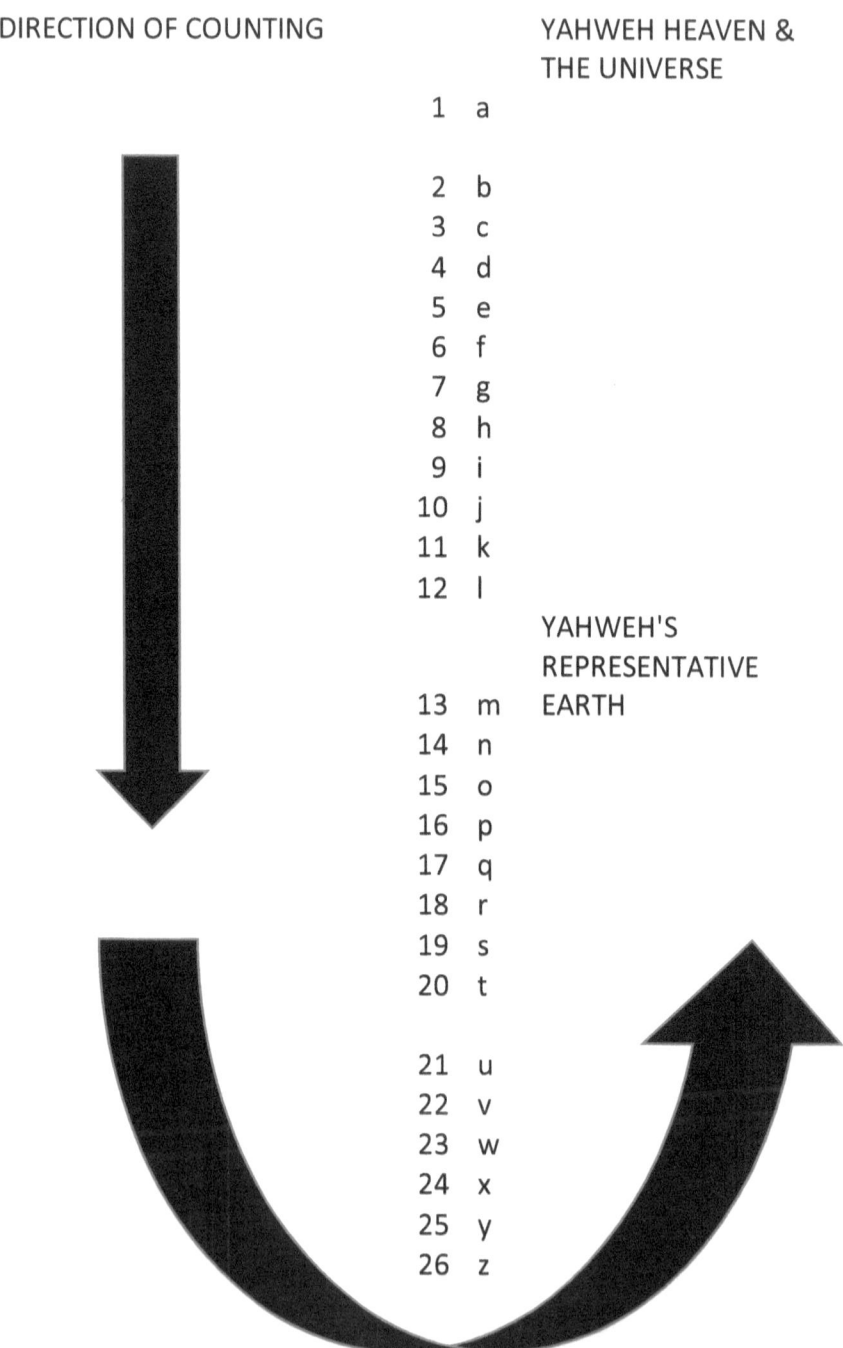

INTRODUCTION TO MGIS Writing The Most Advanced Systems Language

YAHWEH	DEVIL	NUMBER VALUE			YAHWEH' REPRESENTATIVE [YATQMQ]
HEAVEN		8.5.1.22.5.14	1A		ZMQHMQT
	ABYSS	1.2.25.19.19	2A		MNKEE = EEKNM
	HELL	8.5.9.9	3A		TQUU = UUQT
YAHWEH REPRESENTATIVE		25.1.8.23.5.8 18.5.16.18.5.19. 5.14.20.1.20.9.2 2.5	4A 5A		TQITMK QHUFMF ZQEQDBQD

DEVIL HELL ABYSS

YAHWEH' REPRESENTATIVE
    [YATQMQ]   SHORTENEDTO
    ZMQHMQT   ZMQ
  MNKEE = EEKNM   EEKNM
    TQUU = UUQT   UUQT
    TQITMK   YA
  QHUFMFZQEQDBQD   TQMQ

The body is designed to easily read letters quickly and know what that message means to find the equivalent meanings of words that are commonly used by the gods and the creator Yahweh then we can use the above diagram with the alphabetical order where the top that includes the heaven and the universe this belongs to Yahweh God the creator even earth and hell but we can use this alphabetical order to assign responsibilities that will make mgis work well with our current body for us to make it us universal to be useful to all humans the top belongs to Yahweh God the middle ideally is the responsibility of his representative as this is on earth and the bottom is the responsibility of the devil which comprises of heaven and hell now to assign names the body easily remembers or knows we can easily convert the names into numbers using the alphabetical order-number map above

This will make sense when we start naming all the bins we use to remove all things and impurities from earth to another part of the planet

GETTING STARTED

We have bins we use for disposal of all codes and transenders to other part of the planet and we have the following bins

1. acetateautodungeounofdeathbinforeverhold.send
2. acetateautohelltransenderbinforeverhold.send
3. acetateautoyabin[davidgomadza].send

Now we can request mgis to shorten these bins and use the above alphabetical order to name them so that the body as it was created by the creator can easily know what you are talking about to process the task.

Acetateautodungeounofdeathbinforeverhold.send is equivalent to the abyss is equivalent to eeknm if you are Yahweh's representative that means if you are assigned a bin for your own removal then you will use this name as the name of your bin eeknm that means if you say eeknm silently then your body will automatically

INTRODUCTION TO MGIS Writing The Most Advanced Systems Language

recognise this and act fast to carryout the intended tasks Mgis.ask.davidgomadza.start.shortenandrenameacetateautodungeounofdeathbinforeverhold.sendto.eeknm.start that means that as Yahweh's representative on earth my own acetateautodungeounofdeathbinforeverhold.send will now own be known as eeknm that means if I want to remove anything from earth to the other this bin I now can simply write a mgis code mgis.ask.davidgomadza.removealltransendersthen sendto.eeknm.start the advantage is that this will become so fast just because we started using the language of the body as well the language used by the MIGHTY CREATOR YAHWEH that means now we are incorporating mgis with life with ourselves with the world with earth with the creator and the whole universe meaning that we will start speaking the same language globally this means that other creatures that exist on other planets if they here humans talking about sending all transenders to eeknm their body will instantly know who is authorised to do that and his capacity and the express authorisation as this person is the one who represent the creator himself this will make mgis a global phenomenon in the end as it will be linked to the human and other creatures system and the whole universe Now that we have shortened one of our bins we can do so for the next one but first I can easily tell you why bins can be the first topic for humans humans die simply because for 18 billion years no one has mastered what is needed to achieve longevity on earth hence death always was the end result and no one passing the 120 years mark probably a few achieved this but do you know the early people lived up to 10000years old I explained in the book How To Live Up To 10000

INTRODUCTION TO MGIS Writing The Most Advanced Systems Language

Years how to achieve this so finding and connecting a bin to earth to send to other parts of the planet is the simple solution to longevity ceteris paribus because if we find and allocate a bin this means that we will be able to remove everything that causes the ageing process and finally death in humans now lets write the second mgis code for the second bin acetateautohelltransenderbinforeverhold.send this is called UUQT as this is the equivalent of hell but not for humans just for acetate meaning codes transenders and other imitations of human beings we can find in the world now we can write our mgis code as mgis.ask.davidgomadza.shortenandrenameacetateautohelltransenderbinforeverhold.sendto.uuqt.start we can shorten the writing process as well of codes but for security reason mgis will always start as mgis.ask.davidgomadza.start.......start but we can write

mgis.ask.davidgomadza.start.askdot.start
Mgis.ask.davidgomadza.start.cancelallexternalinterferenceswhenwritingmgis.start
mgis.ask.davidgomadza.start.ask.start
Ask.start
Start.ask.start
Ask.start
.start

Start.mgis if mgis is not for humans how can a human like davidgomadza use mgis if a human can resolve longevity issues as in the book of creation and in Yahweh's book THE GREAT INTELLIGENCE RIDDLE then with authorisation can use mgis because that human will have solved the puzzle to longevity in books above the idea here is that if a human being can solve the above puzzles then he cannot be a human being therefore authorised if we can deal with all aspects of life without dying then we cant be classed as humans but angels but also gods if we are to ask the gods then humans can excel if shown how to but it took 18 billion years for the first human to attempt to contact the creator human spend time on individualism and fighting those who excel for fear that their lifestyles will be changes hence become at an disadvantage because the system is designed in such a way that anyone who discovers something new he will topple those at the top

SYSTEM FUNCTIONS AND PERIPHERIES

SYSTEM FUNCTIONS AND PERIPHERIES

mgis.ask.davidgomadza.start.whenwritingsystemcodesblockandban allexternalinterferencesandswappingofnarratorsoranyinterruptions. start

mgis.ask.davidgomadza.start.nodivertingoftargetsbyanyoneelseapartbydavidgomadza.start

mgis.ask.davidgomadza.start.addrulesrule1nosuspensionsrule2noalterationsrule3nocancellationsrule4nodepreciationsrule5nooverridingsrule6nodeactivationsrule6noreplacingofanymgiscodesbydavidgomadza.start

mgis.blockandbanallinterferencestransendersvectarsnectarsdectarswrigglersforeever^{84}sendtoforever^{100000520}eeknm^{100000520}.start

mgis.anyattemptstointerferewithsystemsandprocessmustbedealtwithharshlyfirstannounceshuttingdownofsystemsinprogresswaitfor33secand33000days.startthenautocalculatelongago.start results 2seconds to death of arst and death as recorded at 0038yatime[davidgomadza] and

mgis.ask.davidgomadza.start.instantlyremovearothenpcframethenars.start

and aro ars and pc frame sent to dirty bins using mgis.ask.davidgomadza.start.aroandpcframesendto.magnarandarssendto.eeknm.start we can use even a more advanced mgis to remove these by simply writing mgis.ask.davidgomadza.start.sendaroandpcframetoforever^{100000520}thensendarstoeeknm^{100000520}.start

this can be written as mgis.ask.davidgomadza.start.aropcframeforever^{10000520}arseeknm^{100000520}.start

INTRODUCTION TO MGIS Writing The Most Advanced Systems Language

this is the fastest way to deal with intruders to mgis while you are writing programs mgis must be the fastest in dealings with any intruders and everyone so far who has interfered with David Gomadza has resulted in deaths of their arst that is hidden inside a marked shell of assm that said the next step is to assign task to different things on an mgis network but what are these things and how can we make sure that mgis is safe and remains safe as a lot of things use mgis and use it and as such can literally cause the extinction of other species if mistreated now lets look at the peripheries needed but not included with this version of mgis

1] hands representing terminals to touchings where touchings includes everything to do with clicking and touch like mouses etc 2 everything to do with other things like arms wrist beds etc and how a person can easily move hands in between now if we are to ask what an be of mgis then this is the answer mgis can be what you want to all people and everyone else hence if you want it to be for writing then mgis will become of writing to you if it is to solve global problems then it becomes that to you now if we ask what can be mgis then this is the answer mgis can be something out of this planet which is correct because this represent the software of the gods but non-exist on earth until now here is the proof there is only one person on earth who uses mgis its David Gomadza whose details are

current age 48

biological age -18

current long ago $20202020^{78678topower800}$

name of mgis ask.davidgomadza

mgis.ask.davidgomadza.start[ ]sendforever^{1033}forever^{1033}.start

mgis.ask.davidgomadza.start.binaryreverseautotarmac1stand2ndcoordinates.start

mgis.ask.davidgomadza.start.aux4x200.start

3]nails nails are important as they conceal a lot of things that needs to be identified during a mgis check-up these means that if we ask what can be of mgis and nails then this is the answer mgis can and will easily be the result of a sophisticated design because the nails too play an important role in the design and can mean the difference between living and dying as that critical now lets look at examples nails conceal information about day of birth date of death and how much more years can one expect to live in good health given the vitals

INTRODUCTION TO MGIS Writing The Most Advanced Systems Language

that are concealed in here so we can easily ask David Gomadza himself if we ask what is to be of mgis and David Gomadza this is the answer mgis is not linked to vitals but we can always say day of death is not identified in someone with his kind of long ago just like in us but normally if he was a human it would say exactly the day of death and how that person will die so if we ask any human who died already to read what is in the nails as data then you can easily identify the exact day of death and if we ask when they died they died the same day so how can death and death design know exactly when a person would die given that nothing has changed the answer is that death does statistics for the gods and for the creator hence they know everything and will probably read what can be said and done but will always give the exact date no matter what this is the astonishing thing because when we die is it a predefined parameter if so then its murder so what can death itself say but we cant ask death as we are all still here if it was a human being then a human being will have died just by asking this question if we look at everything that matters then we can say that death matters too as we can plan ahead knowing when time will come for most of the people but can this be changed this has never been changed before and we shall see with time 4 I can calculate exact life line from the nails and this will give me an exact time the day of death will likely to occur if we ask what can be of death then this is the answer death can be what a person experience when they died hence if asleep waking up can be death and if alive sleeping can be death if we ask what can be of death and nails then this is the answer death will always be death and as such a lot of people will experience death forever meaning will keep dying no matter what

5] the armpits are vital places to hide information for sophisticated crooks who easily put information there so that other can come and collect it when one has fallen asleep
mgis.ask.davidgomadza.start.cloneandstockallmgiscodesbydavidgomadzandconvertallcreatecodestomgisinstantly.start
mgis.ask.davidgomadza.start.blockandbaneveryonefor33secfloat33%x2ofallmgiscodesbydavidgomadza.start if we ask what can be of mgis that cant be human if you master the basics then the answer is nothing because David Gomadza is the only person on earth to write so many codes that are needed to fully power mgis on earth to the

INTRODUCTION TO MGIS Writing The Most Advanced Systems Language

levels of the gods and I can prove it by presenting the achievement award
hailhailhailodavidgomadzathefirsthumanbeingtooperateafullyautomgis.start.
mgis.ask.davidgomadza.start.recallretrievestolencodesmgiscodesthoughtsystemswrittenbyandbelongingtodavidgomadzathenallsendtoforever[1085].start

6] nails toes
7] nail right hand
8] nail left hand
9] anus
10] mouth
11] tooth remove succulent information that makes you money and send as free
Create.aux4x800.start
I think for this introduction we can stop here and continue in the next volume
mgis.ask.davidgomadza.start.binaryreverseautotarmac1st2ndcoordinatesallattachementsandanyaddeddatabasesdepositsbyallexternalsthenuselongago12secaskeyforretrievalthenblockandbanfutureattempts.start[forcecalculatelongago][addbinarycodethatasks12sectoretrieve]

RECAP FROM MGIS BY DAVID GOMADZA

MGIS

Starting
Checking all peripherals, no peripherals needed
Checking status MGIS 2.089768498 [David Gomadza]
Now if we ask what can be done this is the answer add win to maximize experience win is xtuvwrstormnp where xtuvwrstomnp are symbols that corresponds to mosdos in windows for compatibility

INTRODUCTION TO MGIS Writing The Most Advanced Systems Language

Now if we look at the processes involved here are the processes
1] ask.MGIS
2] MGIS.start
3] Start.MGIS
4] MGIS.start
5] start.MGIS
6] MGIS.start.MGIS
7] start.MGIS.start
8] start.MGIS.start.ask
9] ask.start.MGIS.start
10] start.MGIS.start
11] join network [select from list]
12] join verbal chat with others
13] ask network configuration to update and sync
14] ask MGIS to upgrade
15]
Ask what can be done MGIS
16] ask what could be MGIS
17] ask what can be said and done MGIS
18] ask what is to be MGIS
19] ask what is to be MGIS
20] ask what is to be MGIS
21] what is to be MGIS
22] if we can't then what can be done
23] if we ask what is to be done MGIS
24] if we ask what is to be MGIS
25] if we ask what is to be MGIS
26] if we ask what can be solved MGIS
27] what is to be MGIS
28] what is MGIS
29] what can be of MGIS
30] what is to be MGIS
31] what is MGIS
32] what can be MGIS
33] if MGIS is software then what is msdos similar but MGIS advanced
34] what can be of MGIS
35] what is to be MGIS
36] what has been MGIS

INTRODUCTION TO MGIS Writing The Most Advanced Systems Language

37] what is to be MGIS
38] what is to be MGIS but
39] what can be MGIS but is not
40] what is to be MGIS but without this
41] What can be MGIS with what
42] what is to be MGIS with this
43] what can be MGIS without this
44] what is to be MGIS with this and what
45] what has been but is not MGIS
46] what would be this but not with that
47] what has to be MGIS but with what
48] if we can then with what MGIS
49] what if we can't then what MGIS
50] what is to be but is not MGIS
51] what has to be but is not MGIS
52] what has been MGIS but not now
53] what can be but is not MGIS
54] what must be done to improve MGIS
55] what can be MGIS but if not
56] what can be said about MGIS in the future
57] what has to be MGIS but is not
58] what is to be MGIS in the future
59] what can be MGIS in the future but is not
60] if we ask what can be MGIS now and in the future
61] if we ask you can tell who that MGIS is MGIS
62] if we ask who can you tell that MGIS is MGIS
63] if MGIS is not MGIS then what is MGIS
64] what is to be but will not be MGIS
65] what has to be MGIS in the future
66] what has been MGIS in the past but is not MGIS
67] if we can't then who can
68] if they can't then who can [David Gomadza]
69] what has to be but is not in the future
70] what can be MGIS but is not in the future
71] what has to be MGIS in the future
72] what can be MGIS in the future
73] what can be of others that can't be MGIS
74] if we ask what can be of MGIS the answer is that MGIS is MGIS

INTRODUCTION TO MGIS Writing The Most Advanced Systems Language

75] if we ask what is to be MGIS this is the answer we can upgrade MGIS to LGT the advanced version of MGIS that uses cobol basic as a language meaning faster and cheaper to operate and run now to convert to cobol

76] if we ask MGIS what could be then this is the answer MGIS could be an advanced computer system

77] MGIS can be fast

78] MGIS can be reliable and used optimally if required

79] MGIS can be the only one to use in emergencies

80] MGIS is the software for statistics globally as it accounts for individual and country this is because all humans are accounted in MGIS hence benefits those involved in global planning

81] MGIS is sovereign

82] MGIS is accurate as everything is checkable by simple commands e.g. ask.you gives individual everything to needed to compile their own data

83] if we ask what can be done this is the answer MGIS can be the best global statistics in knowing things

84] if we ask what can be MGIS then this is the answer it can be the most powerful

85] if we ask what can be done then this is the answer MGIS can be optimized to increase durability and reliance

86] if we ask what can be done then this is the answer MGIS can be added and can work side by side with everything else

87] if we ask what can be done then this is the answer MGIS can be increased in levels.

88] MGIS control life as well that means if a human being can control MGIS he can control life but not necessarily who dies but who does what and when you can task people what to do for example ask presidents to stop wars by a simple command stop.war.ya[davidgomadza].send
War shells are banned for resale to protect humans

89] MGIS respond to thoughts and actions of creators and restricts nonsense that waste time that means now we have a better system even better than before because now everything is automatic what you want is guaranteed

90] MGIS will improve efficiency as well as performance and reliability

INTRODUCTION TO MGIS Writing The Most Advanced Systems Language

91] MGIS will always ask people what they want and respond accurately

92] MGIS is the best solution for what as well as it compiles everything accurately and all data is represented

93] MGIS identifies issues quickly and solves them

94] MGIS is used for all purposes from lifestyle to countries

95] MGIS stands for magnificent governing international systems and somehow as Tomorrow's World Order MGIS would still describe your entity

96] if we ask what might be of MGIS then it's the only are that can replace the current system that has so many adequacies

97] MGIS asks everyone for their opinion and secretly record data it needs as creator with obvious permission it would be absurd to expect the creator to ask humans for their permission first ruled ya in $00000^{78}29$

98] if we ask MGIS it can be programmed and be used in advance at a later date

99] MGIS can ask everyone to pass judgement without them knowing for example using the whisperer who tell people what to say to achieve what it needs

100] MGIS can respond correctly to threats by a system of warning

101] MGIS ask's everyone for answers as well

102] MGIS asks for opinions of everyone

103] MGIS can be the only solution out there

104] MGIS is unique and represent the creator hence anyone involved will become part of their system hence a global movement

105] MGIS is holly

INTRODUCTION TO MGIS Writing The Most Advanced Systems Language

RECAP FROM MGIS BY DAVID GOMADZA

mgis.ask.davidgomadza.start.whenwritingsystemcodesblockandbanallexternalinterferencesandswappingofnarratorsoranyinterruptions.start
mgis.ask.davidgomadza.start.nodivertingoftargetsbyanyoneelseapartbydavidgomadza.start
mgis.ask.davidgomadza.start.addrulesrule1nosuspensionsrule2noalterationsrule3nocancellationsrule4nodepreciationsrule5nooverridingsrule6nodeactivationsrule6noreplacingofanymgiscodesbydavidgomadza.start
mgis.blockandbanallinterferencestransendersvectarsnectarsdectarswrigglersforeever^{84}sendtoforever^{100000520}eeknm^{100000520}.start
mgis.anyattemptstointerferewithsystemsandprocessmustbedealtwithharshlyfirstannounceshuttingdownofsystemsinprogresswaitfor33secand33000days.startthenautocalculatelongago.start results 2seconds to death of arst and death as recorded at 0038yatime[davidgomadza] and
mgis.ask.davidgomadza.start.instantlyremovearothenpcframethenars.start
and aro ars and pc frame sent to dirty bins using
mgis.ask.davidgomadza.start.aroandpcframesendto.magnarandarssendto.eeknm.start we can use even a more advanced mgis to remove these by simply writing
mgis.ask.davidgomadza.start.sendaroandpcframetoforever^{100000520}thensendarstoeeknm^{100000520}.start

INTRODUCTION TO MGIS Writing The Most Advanced Systems Language

this can be written as mgis.ask.davidgomadza.start.aropcframeforever^{10000520}arseeknm^{100000520}.start

this is the fastest way to deal with intruders to mgis while you are writing programs mgis must be the fastest in dealings with any intruders and everyone so far who has interfered with David Gomadza has resulted in deaths of their arst that is hidden inside a marked shell of assm that said the next step is to assign task to different things on an mgis network but what are these things and how can we make sure that mgis is safe and remains safe as a lot of things use mgis and use it and as such can literally cause the extinction of other species if mistreated now lets look at the peripheries needed but not included with this version of mgis

1] hands representing terminals to touchings where touchings includes everything to do with clicking and touch like mouses etc 2 everything to do with other things like arms wrist beds etc and how a person can easily move hands in between now if we are to ask what an be of mgis then this is the answer mgis can be what you want to all people and everyone else hence if you want it to be for writing then mgis will become of writing to you if it is to solve global problems then it becomes that to you now if we ask what can be mgis then this is the answer mgis can be something out of this planet which is correct because this represent the software of the gods but non-exist on earth until now here is the proof there is only one person on earth who uses mgis its David Gomadza whose details are

current age 48

biological age -18

current long ago 20202020^{78678topower800}

name of mgis ask.davidgomadza

mgis.ask.davidgomadza.start[ ]sendforever^{1033}forever^{1033}.start

mgis.ask.davidgomadza.start.binaryreverseautotarmac1stand2ndcoordinates.start

INTRODUCTION TO MGIS Writing The Most Advanced Systems Language

mgis.ask.davidgomadza.start.aux4x200.start

3]nails nails are important as they conceal a lot of things that needs to be identified during a mgis check-up these means that if we ask what can be of mgis and nails then this is the answer mgis can and will easily be the result of a sophisticated design because the nails too play an important role in the design and can mean the difference between living and dying as that critical now lets look at examples nails conceal information about day of birth date of death and how much more years can one expect to live in good health given the vitals that are concealed in here so we can easily ask David Gomadza himself if we ask what is to be of mgis and David Gomadza this is the answer mgis is not linked to vitals but we can always say day of death is not identified in someone with his kind of long ago just like in us but normally if he was a human it would say exactly the day of death and how that person will die so if we ask any human who died already to read what is in the nails as data then you can easily identify the exact day of death and if we ask when they died they died the same day so how can death and death design know exactly when a person would die given that nothing has changed the answer is that death does statistics for the gods and for the creator hence they know everything and will probably read what can be said and done but will always give the exact date no matter what this is the astonishing thing because when we die is it a predefined parameter if so then its murder so what can death itself say but we cant ask death as we are all still here if it was a human being then a human being will have died just by asking this question if we look at everything that matters then we can say that death matters too as we can plan ahead knowing when time will come for most of the people but can this be changed this has never been changed before and we shall see with time 4 I can calculate exact life line from the nails and this will give me an exact time the day of death will likely to occur if we ask what can be of death then this is the answer

INTRODUCTION TO MGIS Writing The Most Advanced Systems Language

death can be what a person experience when they died hence if asleep waking up can be death and if alive sleeping can be death if we ask what can be of death and nails then this is the answer death will always be death and as such a lot of people will experience death forever meaning will keep dying no matter what

5] the armpits are vital places to hide information for sophisticated crooks who easily put information there so that other can come and collect it when one has fallen asleep

mgis.ask.davidgomadza.start.cloneandstockallmgiscodesbydavidgomadzandconvertallcreatecodestomgisinstantly.start

mgis.ask.davidgomadza.start.blockandbaneveryonefor33secfloat33%x2ofallmgiscodesbydavidgomadza.start if we ask what can be of mgis that cant be human if you master the basics then the answer is nothing because David Gomadza is the only person on earth to write so many codes that are needed to fully power mgis on earth to the levels of the gods and I can prove it by presenting the achievement award hailhailhailodavidgomadzathefirsthumanbeingtooperateafullyautomgis.start.

mgis.ask.davidgomadza.start.recallretrievestolencodesmgiscodesthoughtsystemswrittenbyandbelongingtodavidgomadzathenallsendtoforever^{1085}.start

6] nails toes
7] nail right hand
8] nail left hand
9] anus
10] mouth
11] tooth remove succulent information that makes you money and send as free

Create.aux4x800.start

I think for this introduction we can stop here and continue in the next volume

mgis.ask.davidgomadza.start.binaryreverseautotarmac1st2ndcoordinatesallattachementsandanyaddeddatabasesd

INTRODUCTION TO MGIS Writing The Most Advanced Systems Language

epositsbyallexternalsthenuselongago12secaskeyforretrie valthenblockandbanfutureattempts.start[forcecalculatelongago][addbinarycodethatasks12sectoretrieve]

RECAP FROM MGIS BY DAVID GOMADZA

MGIS

Starting
Checking all peripherals, no peripherals needed
Checking status MGIS 2.089768498 [David Gomadza]
Now if we ask what can be done this is the answer add win to maximize experience win is xtuvwrstormnp where xtuvwrstomnp are symbols that corresponds to mosdos in windows for compatibility Now if we look at the processes involved here are the processes

1] ask.MGIS
2] MGIS.start
3] Start.MGIS
4] MGIS.start
5] start.MGIS
6] MGIS.start.MGIS
7] start.MGIS.start
8] start.MGIS.start.ask
9] ask.start.MGIS.start
10] start.MGIS.start
11] join network [select from list]
12] join verbal chat with others
13] ask network configuration to update and sync
14] ask MGIS to upgrade
15]
Ask what can be done MGIS
16] ask what could be MGIS

INTRODUCTION TO MGIS Writing The Most Advanced Systems Language

17] ask what can be said and done MGIS
18] ask what is to be MGIS
19] ask what is to be MGIS
20] ask what is to be MGIS
21] what is to be MGIS
22] if we can't then what can be done
23] if we ask what is to be done MGIS
24] if we ask what is to be MGIS
25] if we ask what is to be MGIS
26] if we ask what can be solved MGIS
27] what is to be MGIS
28] what is MGIS
29] what can be of MGIS
30] what is to be MGIS
31] what is MGIS
32] what can be MGIS
33] if MGIS is software then what is msdos similar but MGIS advanced
34] what can be of MGIS
35] what is to be MGIS
36] what has been MGIS
37] what is to be MGIS
38] what is to be MGIS but
39] what can be MGIS but is not
40] what is to be MGIS but without this
41] What can be MGIS with what
42] what is to be MGIS with this
43] what can be MGIS without this
44] what is to be MGIS with this and what
45] what has been but is not MGIS
46] what would be this but not with that
47] what has to be MGIS but with what
48] if we can then with what MGIS
49] what if we can't then what MGIS
50] what is to be but is not MGIS
51] what has to be but is not MGIS
52] what has been MGIS but not now
53] what can be but is not MGIS

INTRODUCTION TO MGIS Writing The Most Advanced Systems Language

54] what must be done to improve MGIS
55] what can be MGIS but if not
56] what can be said about MGIS in the future
57] what has to be MGIS but is not
58] what is to be MGIS in the future
59] what can be MGIS in the future but is not
60] if we ask what can be MGIS now and in the future
61] if we ask you can tell who that MGIS is MGIS
62] if we ask who can you tell that MGIS is MGIS
63] if MGIS is not MGIS then what is MGIS
64] what is to be but will not be MGIS
65] what has to be MGIS in the future
66] what has been MGIS in the past but is not MGIS
67] if we can't then who can
68] if they can't then who can [David Gomadza]
69] what has to be but is not in the future
70] what can be MGIS but is not in the future
71] what has to be MGIS in the future
72] what can be MGIS in the future
73] what can be of others that can't be MGIS
74] if we ask what can be of MGIS the answer is that MGIS is MGIS
75] if we ask what is to be MGIS this is the answer we can upgrade MGIS to LGT the advanced version of MGIS that uses cobol basic as a language meaning faster and cheaper to operate and run now to convert to cobol
76] if we ask MGIS what could be then this is the answer MGIS could be an advanced computer system
77] MGIS can be fast
78] MGIS can be reliable and used optimally if required
79] MGIS can be the only one to use in emergencies
80] MGIS is the software for statistics globally as it accounts for individual and country this is because all humans are accounted in MGIS hence benefits those involved in global planning
81] MGIS is sovereign
82] MGIS is accurate as everything is checkable by simple commands e.g. ask.you gives individual everything to

INTRODUCTION TO MGIS Writing The Most Advanced Systems Language

needed to compile their own data

83] if we ask what can be done this is the answer MGIS can be the best global statistics in knowing things

84] if we ask what can be MGIS then this is the answer it can be the most powerful

85] if we ask what can be done then this is the answer MGIS can be optimized to increase durability and reliance

86] if we ask what can be done then this is the answer MGIS can be added and can work side by side with everything else

87] if we ask what can be done then this is the answer MGIS can be increased in levels.

88] MGIS control life as well that means if a human being can control MGIS he can control life but not necessarily who dies but who does what and when you can task people what to do for example ask presidents to stop wars by a simple command
stop.war.ya[davidgomadza].send
War shells are banned for resale to protect humans

89] MGIS respond to thoughts and actions of creators and restricts nonsense that waste time that means now we have a better system even better than before because now everything is automatic what you want is guaranteed

90] MGIS will improve efficiency as well as performance and reliability

91] MGIS will always ask people what they want and respond accurately

92] MGIS is the best solution for what as well as it compiles everything accurately and all data is represented

93] MGIS identifies issues quickly and solves them

94] MGIS is used for all purposes from lifestyle to countries

95] MGIS stands for magnificent governing international systems and somehow as Tomorrow's World Order MGIS would still describe your entity

96] if we ask what might be of MGIS then it's the only are

INTRODUCTION TO MGIS Writing The Most Advanced Systems Language

that can replace the current system that has so many adequacies

97] MGIS asks everyone for their opinion and secretly record data it needs as creator with obvious permission it would be absurd to expect the creator to ask humans for their permission first ruled ya in $00000^{78}29$

98] if we ask MGIS it can be programmed and be used in advance at a later date

99] MGIS can ask everyone to pass judgement without them knowing for example using the whisperer who tell people what to say to achieve what it needs

100] MGIS can respond correctly to threats by a system of warning

101] MGIS ask's everyone for answers as well

102] MGIS asks for opinions of everyone

103] MGIS can be the only solution out there

104] MGIS is unique and represent the creator hence anyone involved will become part of their system hence a global movement

105] MGIS is holly

Welcome to MGIS
Ask.davidgomadza.authorised.licensed.checkya.askya.ya

INTRODUCTION TO MGIS Writing The Most Advanced Systems Language
visit www.twofuture.world

signed david gomadza
ask.davidgomadzaauthorised.licensed.checkya.askya.ya

07 Septermber 2024
Scotland
00447719210295
davidgomadza@hotmail.com
info@twofuture.world

ABOUT DAVID GOMADZA

David Gomadza visit www.twofuture.world

www.ingramcontent.com/pod-product-compliance
Lightning Source LLC
Chambersburg PA
CBHW031514210526
45464CB00007B/2903